WHAT DO YOU DO?

A GUIDE TO THE CLASSES OF THE LARP WORLD

Authored by High Priestess
Aesia of the Angel Realm

Introduction

This tome details every class which may be taken up by people within the world of Fantasy LARP Oxfordshire. The knowledge here is based on what has been seen, and may not be correct for every individual.

This tome also contains the abilities and traits of each class known to us. This may be helpful in combat, for detecting your enemies' weakness.

At the end of this tome is a list of known items which are useable in the world. This list is in no way exhaustive and contains only the most basic of items. Rare and legendary items can be won during games.

1. Melee Classes

1.1 Warrior

Your standard warrior class.

Strength +5

Speed +2

Weapons: One or two-handed melee.

1.2 Beserker

Not-so standard warrior class. They fight with less advanced weaponry and use brute force to win.

Strength +7

Weapons: One or two-handed melee.

1.3   Rogue

Rogues use speed and subtlety to hit the enemy before they even knew they were there.

Strength +1

Speed +10

Subtlety +7

Weapons: Use one or two single-hand melee weapons, and poison.

1.4   Swordsman/Samurai

These holy swordsmen let honour fuel their rage, and fight with the power and speed of a thousand men. Their blade may only rest once drenched in the blood of their enemies.

Strength +12

Speed +6

Wisdom +2

Weapons: Any sword (Nodachi gives +2 on every skill to samurais).

1.5   Monk

Monks use their wisdom and speed to destroy their enemy quickly and subtly.

Wisdom +5

Speed +10

Strength +5

Weapons: Any Staff.

1.6   Paladin

These holy warriors are a blend between a cleric and a warrior. They use a single blade and a holy shield to protect and defend.

Intelligence +3

Wisdom +3

Strength +5

Charisma +2

Weapons: Any one-handed, plus shield.

1.7   Ninja

A ninja fights with speed and subtlety, using both melee and ranged attacks. They fight with their own hands, and with sharp ranged attack weapons. They are a cross between a Rogue and a Monk.

Speed +15

Wisdom +5

Strength +8

Aim +15

Weapons: Throwing knives, throwing stars, staff.

1.8 Knight

The chivalrous knight fights with sword and shield in hand.

Strength +9

Speed +3

Wisdom +4

Charisma +8

Weapons: Any sword.

1.9   Fighter

The fighter class use hand-to-hand combat to take down their enemy.

Strength +10

Speed +8

Aim +5

Weapons: None.

2. Caster Classes

2.1 Cleric

Clerics fight using holy spells.

Intelligence +6

Wisdom +5

Weapons: Any magic weaponry.

2.2   Necromancer

Necromancers raise the dead and use them to do their bidding. When you fight a necromancer, you're fighting an undead army.

Intelligence +3

Proficiency +4

Weapons: Any magic weaponry.

2.3   Sorcerer/Witch

Sorcerers, sorceresses and witches all fight using darker spells, such as hexes and chaos magic, all of which affect their opponent over time, rather than one single hit of damage. Some magic lasts only a few minutes, but hexes and curses can last days, weeks, or even indefinitely.

Intelligence +2

Wisdom +2

Proficiency +2

Weapons: Any magic weaponry.

2.4 Druid

Druids fight using the power of nature. They can call upon the animals or the spirits in the forest to fight for them, or draw on the power of a specific animal to strengthen them. A druid can only have one animal that they can draw upon, which is chosen at their initiation rites.

Wisdom +10

Intelligence +4

Weapons: Any magic weaponry.

2.5   Wizard/Mage

Mages and wizards are just your standard magic-users. They can specialise in one specific type of magic, or know a small amount about every type of magic.

Intelligence +5

Wisdom +5

Proficiency +10

Weapons: Any magic weaponry.

2.6 Warlock

Warlocks are greedy and selfish, using spells that drain magic and life from their opponent, sometimes giving it back to themselves. They can also summon a dark spirit to lurk over the opponent, which drains their life slowly over time.

Intelligence +5

Wisdom +1

Weapons: Any magic weaponry.

2.7   Elementalist/Shaman

Elementalists and shamans use the powers of nature to take down their enemies. They can control Water, Earth, Air and Fire. They can also use the meditation ability whilst near a body of water to heal their own injuries.

Intelligence +5

Wisdom +6

3. Ranged Classes

3.1　Archer/Ranger/Hunter

Hunters, Rangers and Archers use the forest to their advantage and slink in the shadows, careful not to let their prey know they are there. They are good survivalists, and are brilliant at setting traps. They are often given the job of being a scout.

Aim +10
Subtlety +5
Speed +5
Weapons: Any ranged weapon.

3.2 *Spearman*

Spearmen throw spears. They have lots of upper body strength.

Aim +7

Strength +5

Weapons: Spear, Javelin.

3.3   *Assassin*

Assassins use their speed and subtlety to snipe their opponent, without a need to be in close range of them. [Often, Assassins possess the secondary trait 'Vampirism', which allows them more speed, subtlety, and the ability to attack at close range, but means they cannot attack during daylight.]

Aim +10
Speed +10
Subtlety +10
Weapons: Any ranged weapon.

3.4   Gunslinger

Gunslingers use cutting-edge engineering to shoot metallic projectiles at high speed, incapacitating their enemy, and sometimes killing with a single shot. Gunslingers are recognised as a ranged class, but their weaponry can also be effective at close range, providing they can get a good shot to a fatal area of the body.

Aim +12
Strength +5
Speed +7
Weapons: Pistol, Revolver.

4.   Healer Classes

4.1   Priest

4.1   Priest

Priests use their holy powers to heal the sick and injured. [It is optional, but priests may be ordained before the game begins, in order to create immersion.]

Intelligence +6

Wisdom +5

Weapons: Any magic weapons.

5. Secondary Classes

5.1 Bard

The role of bard is given to one character with good charisma and a delightful singing voice. They use their cheerful ballads and shanties to boost the team morale, and narrate the adventure.

Team morale +10

Charisma +4

Team Community +5

Items: Musical items.

5.2   Navigator

The role of a navigator is to ensure their team does not get lost during their adventure. [This role is reserved for players who know the area well, or have previous experience navigating, e.g. Scouts/Cadets. It is important that every team has a navigator, for health and safety purposes.]

Intelligence +4

Items: Compass.

5.3   Bandit

Bandits are exceptional thieves. Their job is to sneak into the opposing teams' camp and gain intel and supplies, without being seen. They are often caught and imprisoned/executed by the opposing team.

Subtlety +5

Items: Satchel.

5.4 Vampire

The Vampire in the team cannot go into daylight, and can only fight in shadows. They are often Assassins but any class can pick up the Vampire trait.

Speed +5

Subtlety +5

Team morale -3

Items: Vial of blood.

5.5   First Aider/Medic

The medic is in charge of dealing with minor wounds and illness that the team healers do not have the time for. [The first aider on the team does not necessarily have to know genuine first aid, as a first aider WILL be on hand in case of emergency, but they MUST carry a first aid kit with them, in case the game's first aider cannot make it there immediately.]

Team Community +5

Team Morale +5

Items: Medic's Satchel.

5.6   Chef

It is the job of the chef to ensure people are eating. [This is important; we will not go OOC to eat, so the Chef must gather their team for food at a certain point to ensure people are not getting dehydrated or hungry.]

Team Community +5

Team Morale +3

Items: Wooden spoon.

5.7   Scout

The scout is in charge of going out into the wilderness to find out where things are, and possibly locate the enemy camp. They may be caught and imprisoned/executed. [Scout should normally be escorted by a gm/marshall to ensure they don't get lost or injured.]

Intelligence +5

Items: Blank map.

5.8 Treasure Hunter

The Treasure Hunter spends all their time when they aren't fighting searching the area for the hidden treasures that await in the wilderness. Treasures include legendary items such as weapons, holdables, and relics.

5.9 Psychic

The team psychic can catch glimpses of the future, which allows the team to plan moves against the opposing team's actions, before they have even been enacted, allowing for a more likely victory. They can also predict weather changes and possible encounters with friends and foes in the area.

Intelligence +4

Wisdom +4

6. Professions

6.1   Alchemist

Alchemists are able to craft potions. As their skills progress they can create rarer and more powerful potions, eventually being able to create their own legendary potions.

6.2   Engineer

Engineers are able to create and maintain technological weaponry, such as guns. As their skill grows, they can create rare powerful weapons, and create their own legendary weapons.

6.3   Blacksmith

Blacksmiths have the skill to maintain all metal weapons. They can also create weapons as their skill grows, and are able to craft their own legendary weapons when their skill reaches its peak.

6.4   Tailor

A tailor has the skill to craft items made from leather or fabric. This includes items such as satchels, and some armor using patterns they find and learn. As their skill grows they are able to create more protective gear, and larger satchels. They can eventually create their own legendary armor.

6.5   Carpenter

A carpenter has the skill to maintain and craft wooden weapons using designs and sketches that they find and learn. Eventually they are able to create their own legendary weapons, such as bows.

6.6   Enchanter

Enchanters imbue weapons and armour with magical qualities, giving extra damage, or extra protection against damage. Examples of enchantments are fire, ice, poison and sharpness for weapons, and barkskin, ironskin and diamondskin for armour.

6.7   *Mentor*

Mentors are able to pass their own learnt skills and other skills on to other people (perhaps for a fee…). In other words, they are able to impart their knowledge and wisdom on to students.

6.8 Linguist

Linguists can learn to understand all languages in the world. They are useful when coming across foreign NPCs.

MELEE WEAPONS	
(One Handed)	**Required Skill:**
Club	Str +10
Handaxe	Str +3
Cutlass	Str +2
Whip	Str +1
Dagger	Str +1
Mace	Str +5
Quarterstaff	Str +6
Glaive (short)	Str +8
Rapier	Str +2
Shortsword	Str +5
Flail	Str +10
Katana	Str +5
Psion Blade	Str +10 (Psion only)
(Two Handed)	**Required Skill:**
Battleaxe	Str +12
Warhammer	Str +12
Glaive (long)	Str +13
Greataxe	Str +15
Greatsword	Str +18
Nodachi	Str +15 (Samurai only)

Longsword	Str +15
Pike	Str +16
Bokken	Str +14
RANGED	**Required Skill:**
Javelin	Aim +10
Spear	Aim +10
Dagger/Throwing Knife	Aim +15
Throwing Stars	Aim +20
Poison Dart/Blowgun	Aim +15
Crossbow	Aim +12
Shortbow	Aim +12
Longbow	Aim +12
Pistol	Aim +15
Revolver	Aim +20
Slingshot	Aim +15
MAGIC WEAPONS	**Required Skill:**
Quarterstaff	Int +10
Crystal Staff	Int +20
Wand	Int +25
Crystal Orb	Int +15
Magic Tome	Int +20
Gemstone	Int +1

Gem Necklace	Int +5
Totem	Int +20
GENERAL ITEMS	**Description:**
Lute	Played by bards to raise team morale. Team Morale +5
Flute	Played by bards to raise team morale. Can be played to calm or hypnotise an enemy. Team Morale +5
Compass	Use this to find your way.
Blank Map	Use to highlight areas of importance.
Wooden Spoon	Hit people over the head. Also used for cooking.
Satchel	Use to store items.
Vial of Blood	Vampires drink this to stay alive.
Medic's Satchel	Contains useful items for healing minor wounds.
Skin of Water	For staying hydrated.
Weapon Repair Kit	For keeping your weapons in good shape.

Bag of Food	To keep you fed.
POTIONS	**Use:**
Potion of Healing	Heals minor injuries and illness. [Arms, lower legs, any illness]
Potion of Curing	Cures illness.

Name:	Age:
Race:	Class: Secondary Class: Profession:
Racial Traits:	Class Traits:

Inborn skills/talents:	Learnt skills/talents:
Intelligence:	**Aim:**
Speed:	**Strength:**
Wisdom:	**Charisma:**
Subtlety/Sneak:	**Proficiency:**

Other Skills:

Armour:	Weapons:

Items:

Team benefits/buffs:	Team disadvantages/debuffs:

History:

Relationships:

Biography: